INSIDE DK GUIDES

INCREDIBLE EARTH

Written by
NICK CLIFFORD

Coral sea fan

A DK PUBLISHING BOOK

Project Editor Roderick Craig
Art Editor Mark Haygarth
Senior art editor Diane Klein
Managing editor Gillian Denton
Managing art editor Julia Harris
US editor Camela Decaire
Picture Research Jo Carlill
Production Charlotte Traill

Photography Andy Crawford, Ranald Mackechnie
Modelmakers Chris Reynolds and the
team at BBC Visual Effects

First American edition, 1996
2 4 6 8 10 9 7 5 3 1

Published in the United States by DK Publishing, Inc.,
95 Madison Avenue, New York, New York 10016
Copyright © 1996 Dorling Kindersley Limited, London
Visit us on the World Wide Web at http://www.dk.com

A CIP catalog record is available from the Library of Congress.
ISBN 0-7894-1013-3

Reproduced in Italy by G.R.B. Graphica, Verona
Printed in Singapore by Toppan

Model showing the
Earth's anatomy

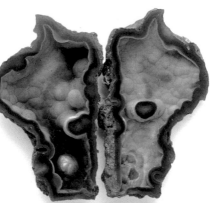

Opal sealed in
a nodule of iron

Saharan fringe-toed lizard

Ice shelf
and icebergs

Emperor penguin,
Antarctic resident

Slice through
a stalagmite

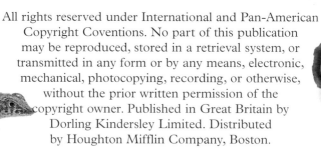

Agate-lined rock cavity

Barrel
cactus

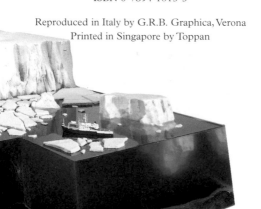

Contents

Tropical fish

Green sea slug

Model of waterfall and river rapids

Crust to core

Imagine a journey to the center of the Earth starting at the crust, which is extremely thin, especially under the oceans. From the crust's rocky strata we derive minerals, ores, fossil fuels, and even heat, which can be harnessed and used in industry. Beneath the crust, unstable shallow layers exist. Movements within these layers are the driving force behind devastating earthquakes and volcanic activity, and they also played a part in the creation of the Earth's vast mountain ranges. We still know little about the Earth's deeper layers, but since the 1960s new techniques have improved our understanding of them – and of the mystery of our planet's evolution over millions of years.

All aboard
The Earth's crust is split into eight sections, or plates, which float on a deeper layer known as the mantle.

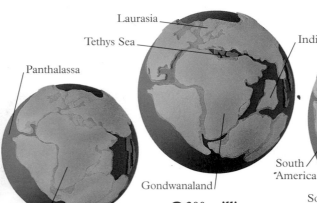

Laurasia
Tethys Sea
India
Panthalassa
South America
Gondwanaland
South Atlantic
Africa
Pangaea

1 **220 million years ago**. A single super-continent floats alone in a vast ocean.

2 **200 million years ago**. The Tethys Sea slowly splits Pangaea into the Gondwanaland and Laurasia masses.

3 **135 million years ago**. Africa and South America appear as Gondwanaland splits.

On the move
The theory of continental drift states that the arrangement of the continents reflects the past movement of the plates on which they lie. So, as the Earth has evolved, the continents, originally joined together, have drifted apart.

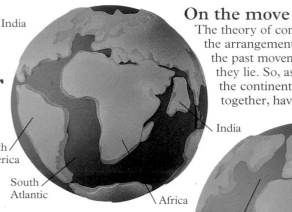

India
Europe
Asia
North Atlantic
Antarctica
Australia

4 **10 million years ago**. The North Atlantic separates Europe and North America. Australia and Antarctica float apart.

Snowy spine
The Himalayas mountain range that dominates Nepal, seen here from space as a long ridge of white peaks, formed as a result of the collision and buckling of the Indian and Asian continental plates. To the right is the high Tibetan Plateau, which was uplifted by the same action.

Meeting plates
As plates move apart along spreading ridges in mid-ocean, new plate material is created by rising lava. Oceanic crust is destroyed where the plates collide. Continental crust "rides" on top of it as it is subducted, or pushed under, into the mantle.

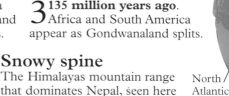

Angry ground
Volcanoes and earthquakes are common in zones of active plate movement.

Old as the sea
All oceanic crust is less than 200 million years old, whereas continental crust is much older.

Subduction zone
Thin oceanic crust melts as it is forced down into the mantle.

Mid-ocean ridge

Points of convergence
Where continental plates crash together, long mountain ranges buckle up along fault lines.

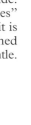

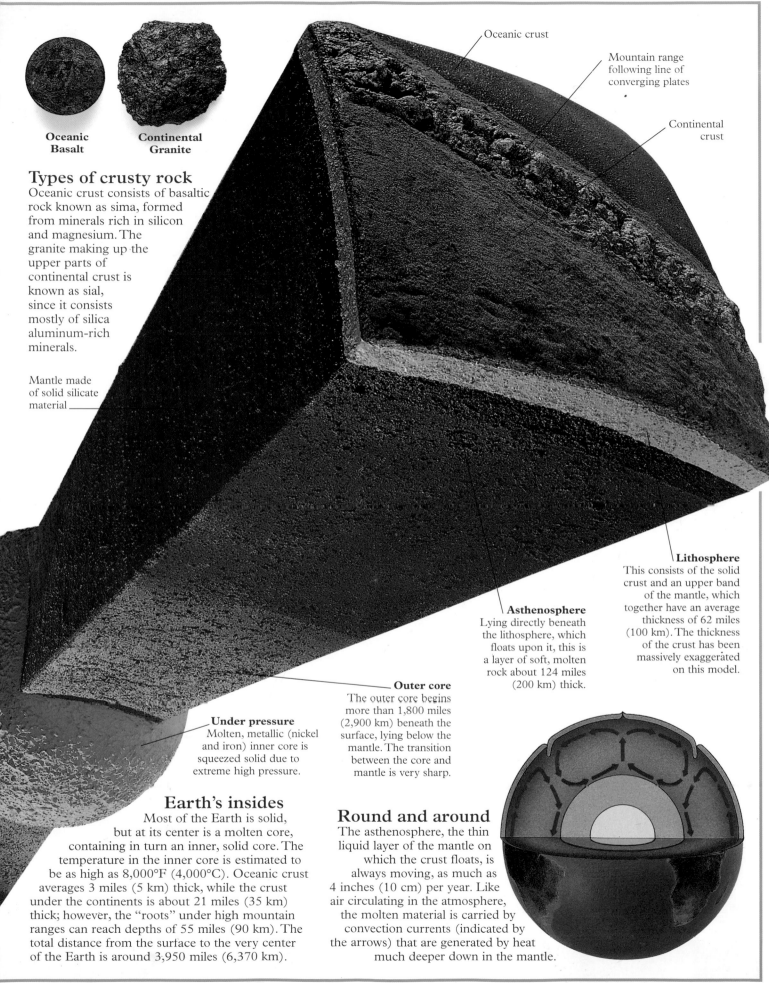

Oceanic Basalt

Continental Granite

Oceanic crust

Mountain range following line of converging plates

Continental crust

Types of crusty rock

Oceanic crust consists of basaltic rock known as sima, formed from minerals rich in silicon and magnesium. The granite making up the upper parts of continental crust is known as sial, since it consists mostly of silica aluminum-rich minerals.

Mantle made of solid silicate material

Lithosphere
This consists of the solid crust and an upper band of the mantle, which together have an average thickness of 62 miles (100 km). The thickness of the crust has been massively exaggerated on this model.

Asthenosphere
Lying directly beneath the lithosphere, which floats upon it, this is a layer of soft, molten rock about 124 miles (200 km) thick.

Outer core
The outer core begins more than 1,800 miles (2,900 km) beneath the surface, lying below the mantle. The transition between the core and mantle is very sharp.

Under pressure
Molten, metallic (nickel and iron) inner core is squeezed solid due to extreme high pressure.

Earth's insides

Most of the Earth is solid, but at its center is a molten core, containing in turn an inner, solid core. The temperature in the inner core is estimated to be as high as 8,000°F (4,000°C). Oceanic crust averages 3 miles (5 km) thick, while the crust under the continents is about 21 miles (35 km) thick; however, the "roots" under high mountain ranges can reach depths of 55 miles (90 km). The total distance from the surface to the very center of the Earth is around 3,950 miles (6,370 km).

Round and around

The asthenosphere, the thin liquid layer of the mantle on which the crust floats, is always moving, as much as 4 inches (10 cm) per year. Like air circulating in the atmosphere, the molten material is carried by convection currents (indicated by the arrows) that are generated by heat much deeper down in the mantle.

Wind and water

Looking at the Earth from space, you see a striking blue planet. This is because more than 70 percent of Earth's surface is covered by water. This watery layer is known as the hydrosphere, and includes the oceans, lakes, rivers, snow, and ice caps. The water that evaporates into the atmosphere forms clouds and is important in regulating the Earth's climate, as are the circulating gyres, or currents, within the oceans. Patterns in the winds and weather systems occurring in the atmosphere, of which hurricanes, or typhoons, and tornadoes are the most violent examples, help in turn to maintain the different climatic zones around the world.

Florida

Gulf of Mexico

Cuba

Eye of the storm
Hurricanes are spiraling, ferocious storm systems in which air currents rise and fall inside a massive cumulonimbus cloud. In the center of the storm is a calm, clear eye. Hurricanes can extend over a wide area, as shown in this enhanced satellite image of Hurricane Andrew, which wreaked havoc in the states of Florida and Louisiana in August 1992.

Troposphere

Stratosphere

Mesosphere

Thermosphere

Earth's atmosphere
The trophosphere is the lowest and densest part of the atmosphere, in which the world's weather occurs. Going up, the air gets thin and cold because there are fewer molecules to absorb solar radiation and trap radiation reflected by the Earth.

Hydrosphere

Exosphere and magnetosphere

Furious funnel
Tornadoes, or whirlwinds, are intense, spiraling windstorms that reach down to the ground from beneath thunderclouds in a characteristic funnel shape. Wind speeds can reach over a savage 250 mph (400 kph). Tornadoes that occur at sea suck up water to form towering waterspouts.

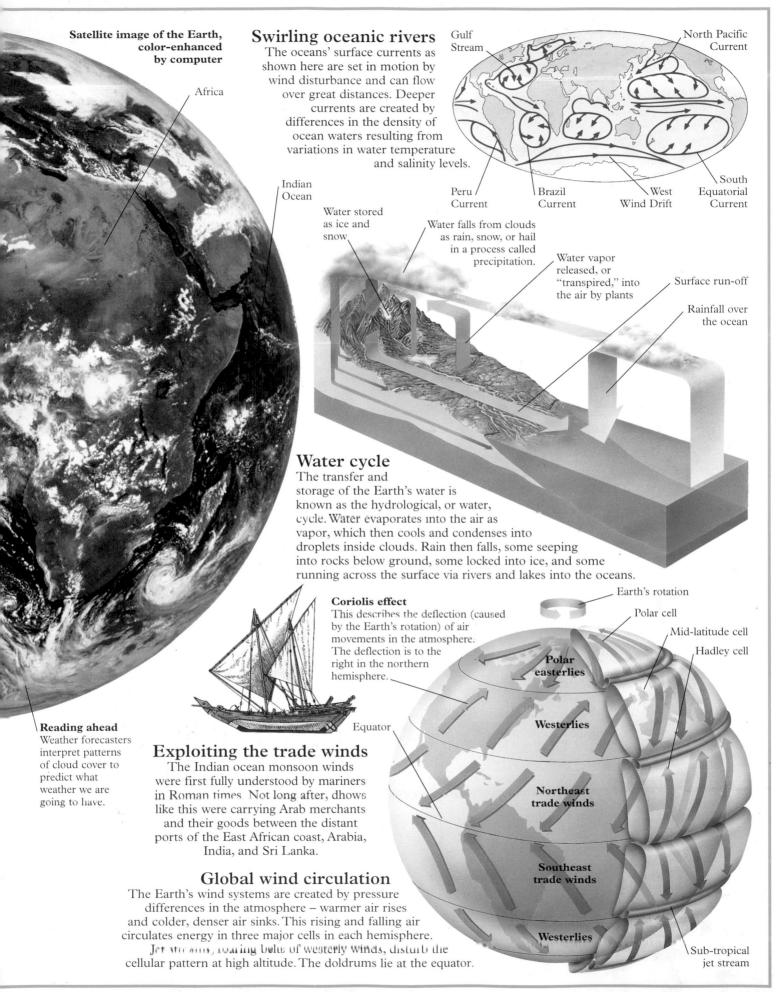

Satellite image of the Earth, color-enhanced by computer

Africa

Indian Ocean

Swirling oceanic rivers

The oceans' surface currents as shown here are set in motion by wind disturbance and can flow over great distances. Deeper currents are created by differences in the density of ocean waters resulting from variations in water temperature and salinity levels.

Gulf Stream

North Pacific Current

Peru Current

Brazil Current

West Wind Drift

South Equatorial Current

Water stored as ice and snow

Water falls from clouds as rain, snow, or hail in a process called precipitation.

Water vapor released, or "transpired," into the air by plants

Surface run-off

Rainfall over the ocean

Water cycle

The transfer and storage of the Earth's water is known as the hydrological, or water, cycle. Water evaporates into the air as vapor, which then cools and condenses into droplets inside clouds. Rain then falls, some seeping into rocks below ground, some locked into ice, and some running across the surface via rivers and lakes into the oceans.

Coriolis effect
This describes the deflection (caused by the Earth's rotation) of air movements in the atmosphere. The deflection is to the right in the northern hemisphere.

Reading ahead
Weather forecasters interpret patterns of cloud cover to predict what weather we are going to have.

Equator

Earth's rotation

Polar cell

Mid-latitude cell

Hadley cell

Polar easterlies

Westerlies

Northeast trade winds

Southeast trade winds

Westerlies

Sub-tropical jet stream

Exploiting the trade winds

The Indian ocean monsoon winds were first fully understood by mariners in Roman times. Not long after, dhows like this were carrying Arab merchants and their goods between the distant ports of the East African coast, Arabia, India, and Sri Lanka.

Global wind circulation

The Earth's wind systems are created by pressure differences in the atmosphere – warmer air rises and colder, denser air sinks. This rising and falling air circulates energy in three major cells in each hemisphere.
Jet streams, roaring belts of westerly winds, disturb the cellular pattern at high altitude. The doldrums lie at the equator.

The fossil record

Fossils are the preserved remains or trace evidence of long-dead flora and fauna, petrified in rocks or buried under peat, ice, or in ancient tree resins. In most cases, only the skeletal parts of organisms survive, the fleshy tissue having rotted away or been replaced by minerals. Why are fossils significant and what do they tell us about the Earth? Organized into a formal system of classification known as the fossil record, they provide important clues to the environment and life on Earth way before history began. The study of fossils, called paleontology, has shown that life originated at least 3.5 billion years ago.

1 An ancient land animal dies and the soft flesh on the carcass starts to decompose where it lies.

2 The intact skeletal remains are rapidly buried by sediment from shallow streams.

3 The material around the fossil turns into rock over millions of years and is covered with other layers.

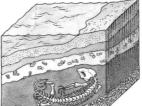

4 As the rock above is eroded away, the fossil is eventually exposed again at the surface.

The fossilization process

This is how organic remains, in this case a small reptile, are typically fossilized. Marine life buried by sediment is exposed later when the seabed is dry, rocky land.

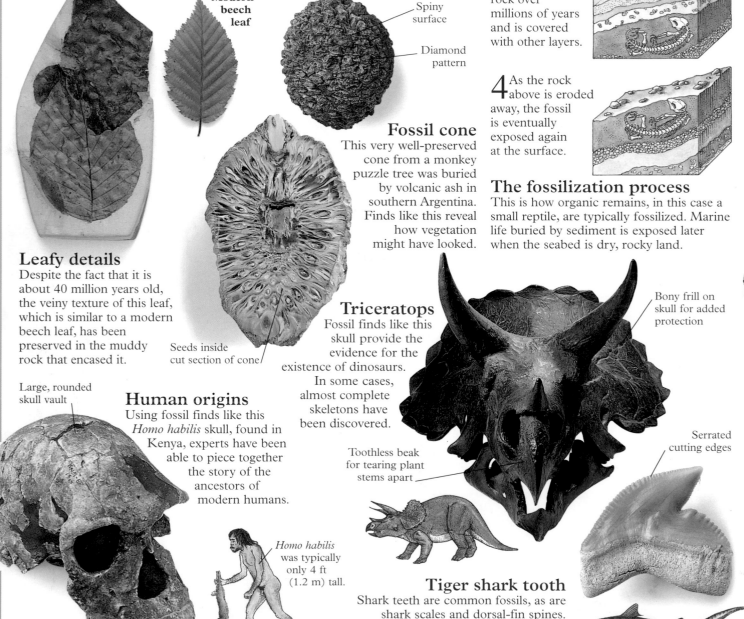

Modern beech leaf

Spiny surface

Diamond pattern

Fossil cone

This very well-preserved cone from a monkey puzzle tree was buried by volcanic ash in southern Argentina. Finds like this reveal how vegetation might have looked.

Seeds inside cut section of cone

Leafy details

Despite the fact that it is about 40 million years old, the veiny texture of this leaf, which is similar to a modern beech leaf, has been preserved in the muddy rock that encased it.

Large, rounded skull vault

Human origins

Using fossil finds like this *Homo habilis* skull, found in Kenya, experts have been able to piece together the story of the ancestors of modern humans.

Homo habilis was typically only 4 ft (1.2 m) tall.

Triceratops

Fossil finds like this skull provide the evidence for the existence of dinosaurs. In some cases, almost complete skeletons have been discovered.

Bony frill on skull for added protection

Toothless beak for tearing plant stems apart

Serrated cutting edges

Tiger shark tooth

Shark teeth are common fossils, as are shark scales and dorsal-fin spines. Sharks have skeletons of cartilage, which do not usually survive to be fossils.

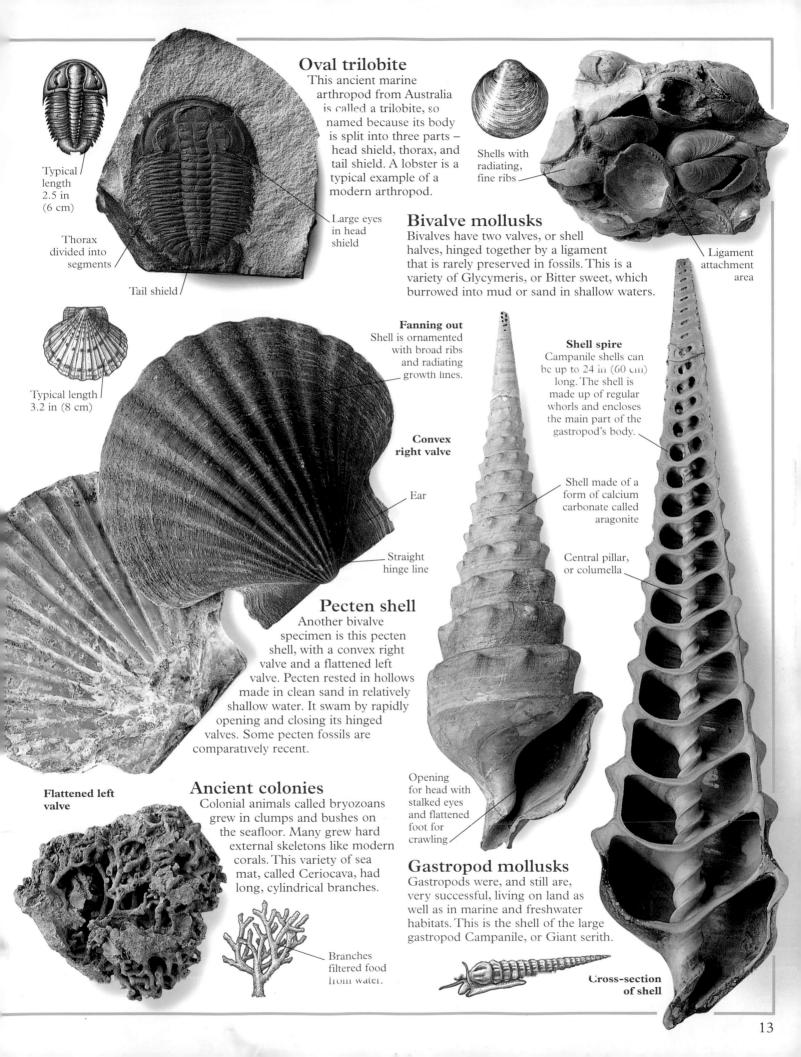

Oval trilobite
This ancient marine arthropod from Australia is called a trilobite, so named because its body is split into three parts – head shield, thorax, and tail shield. A lobster is a typical example of a modern arthropod.

Typical length 2.5 in (6 cm)

Thorax divided into segments

Tail shield

Large eyes in head shield

Shells with radiating, fine ribs

Ligament attachment area

Bivalve mollusks
Bivalves have two valves, or shell halves, hinged together by a ligament that is rarely preserved in fossils. This is a variety of Glycymeris, or Bitter sweet, which burrowed into mud or sand in shallow waters.

Fanning out
Shell is ornamented with broad ribs and radiating growth lines.

Shell spire
Campanile shells can be up to 24 in (60 cm) long. The shell is made up of regular whorls and encloses the main part of the gastropod's body.

Typical length 3.2 in (8 cm)

Convex right valve

Ear

Shell made of a form of calcium carbonate called aragonite

Straight hinge line

Central pillar, or columella

Pecten shell
Another bivalve specimen is this pecten shell, with a convex right valve and a flattened left valve. Pecten rested in hollows made in clean sand in relatively shallow water. It swam by rapidly opening and closing its hinged valves. Some pecten fossils are comparatively recent.

Flattened left valve

Ancient colonies
Colonial animals called bryozoans grew in clumps and bushes on the seafloor. Many grew hard external skeletons like modern corals. This variety of sea mat, called Ceriocava, had long, cylindrical branches.

Opening for head with stalked eyes and flattened foot for crawling

Branches filtered food from water.

Gastropod mollusks
Gastropods were, and still are, very successful, living on land as well as in marine and freshwater habitats. This is the shell of the large gastropod Campanile, or Giant serith.

Cross-section of shell

13

Violent earthquakes

These destructive, terrifying natural disasters are generated by sudden movements deep in the Earth's crust. Enormous pressure builds up in the rocks along fault lines, found all around the boundaries between crustal plates. When the rocks finally snap apart under the stress, the resulting shock waves tear through the land as they travel, often wreaking havoc great distances away. Unfortunately, predicting where and when an earthquake is going to strike is an imprecise science. In danger zones people must always be prepared, and buildings need to be specially designed to withstand the shocks.

Earth crack
The source of the worst earthquakes in the US has been the San Andreas fault system, seen here spanning the Carrizo Plain in the center of California. The distinct kink in the course of each river gulley clearly shows the sliding movement along the fault line.

Types of faults
There are five basic fault types, shown left. Faults can range in size from small cracks to entire mountain ranges and plateaus.

Reverse fault

Normal fault

Horst

Long, narrow block uplifted between parallel normal faults

Rift valley

Long, narrow, sunken block between parallel normal faults

Transform fault

Urban chaos
The power of an earthquake is measured on the Richter scale. Those measuring 8 and above are especially destructive. The damage in urban areas is often made worse by fires, fallen power cables, and ruptured pipes.

Watch your head
Many deaths and injuries are caused by falling masonry and rubble as buildings cave in.

Telephone lines snap and fall.

Gaping holes appear where loose earth liquifies.

Caught off guard

Charleston, South Carolina, was hit by a quake in 1886. The city lies in an almost quake-free zone, so noone was prepared for it. Earthquakes can happen on any fault line at any time.

Weak construction

These houses in San Francisco were built about 75 years ago, on reclaimed land in the Marina district. During the 1989 earthquake, some literally slipped off their foundations.

Fires and explosions occur where gas pipes burst and electricity cables hit the ground.

Earthquakes can be terrifying for drivers on the road.

Freeway foldup

One of the many tragic scenes in the aftermath of the 1989 San Francisco Loma Prieta quake was the surprising collapse of this elevated section of the Nimitz Freeway. A number of motorists were killed.

Built to last
Buildings with stronger foundations or flexible structures tend to remain intact, although windows are likely to shatter.

Folds form in the ground as the earth heaves.

Fault line

Gathering momentum
Tsunami travels at great speed in a low, broad sweep across the deep ocean surface. Its height increases dramatically as it enters a shallower coastal zone.

Walls of water

Earthquakes that occur far beneath the oceans can cause towering tidal waves, or tsunamis. These can reach more than 197 ft (60 m) high when they hit shallow water and cause catastrophic flooding as they batter the shoreline.

Focal point of quake, or epicenter, located along fault in ocean floor

Volcanoes

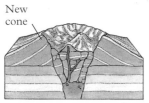

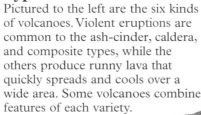

Perhaps the most awe-inspiring and menacing features of the Earth's surface, volcanoes have long represented the mighty power of nature and the gods. Forming above pipelike vents or fissures through which magma or molten rock is forced to the surface, there are, today, around 600 volcanoes on land. Some are active, some dormant, and many more exist in the depths of the oceans. Eruptions can be either violent, ejecting huge amounts of lava, ash, and gas high into the sky, or much gentler, oozing long flows of runny lava.

Road to nowhere
Massive lava flows destroy everything in their path, like the village that once lay at the end of this road near Mount Kilauea volcano in Hawaii.

New cone

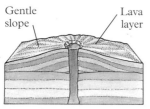

Caldera (crater) volcano

Gentle slope   **Lava layer**

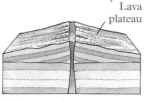

Basic shield volcano

Lava plateau

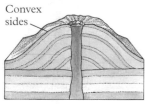

Fissure volcano

Convex sides

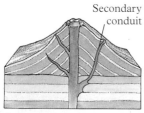

Dome volcano

Secondary conduit

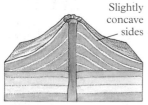

Composite volcano

Slightly concave sides

Ash-cinder volcano

Types of volcanoes
Pictured to the left are the six kinds of volcanoes. Violent eruptions are common to the ash-cinder, caldera, and composite types, while the others produce runny lava that quickly spreads and cools over a wide area. Some volcanoes combine features of each variety.

Flattened out
Repeated lava flows bury surrounding land and can form an extensive volcanic plateau over millions of years.

Rough surface
The barren sides and base of the cone are littered with brittle lumps of cooled lava, ash, and pumice stone.

Layer upon layer
Rings of ash and rock from successive eruptions build up the steep sides of the volcano cone over time.

Smaller ash cinders

Bite-sized lava fragments

Blown to pieces
The ferocity of escaping magma gases pulverizes the rock at the top of a volcanic vent. The ejected material is know as tephra and varies in size from gravelly chunks to vast "bombs" as big as houses.

Ash dust

Fiery furnace
This model represents an active composite volcano with a large central vent and some dykes, or secondary conduits. Its steep-sided cone is built up in layers of ash and acidic lava that correspond to different phases of eruption.

Heart of fire
Central vent spews out ash, sulfurous gases, and fireballs of molten rock.

Pillar of ash
The eruption of Mount St. Helen's in Washington, in May 1980, ejected a column of fine dust 13 miles (20 km) high. Gas and ash raced down its sides at huge speeds, devastating land 16 miles (25 km) away.

Side eruption
Lava pours out of a dyke, or secondary conduit, topped by a small cone.

Patch of yellow sulfur crystals

Lava "sill"
A channel of lava squeezed up between older layers, forming a band of black, glassy obsidian rock called a sill as it cooled.

Trees catch fire as lava approaches.

"Pahoehoe" flow
A lava flow surface covered with ropy ripples is called by their Hawaiian name.

Bulldozing ahead
New dyke of lava gradually forces its way up, under enormous pressure, toward the surface.

Wings of flame
Curtains of molten rock branch out from magma chamber.

Raging torrent
The eruption of Ruiz Volcano in Colombia, in November 1985, caused a slide of melted snow and ash to charge down a canyon and destroy the distant city of Armero, killing 22,000 people.

Main magma chamber

Geyser fields

Otherwise known as hydrothermal areas, geyser fields are home to spectacular phenomena including boiling hot springs, vents spitting out jets of sulfurous gas, cascading sinter terraces, and bubbling mud pools. Geysers, however, are the stars of the show, erupting water and steam in regular cycles. Geyser fields occur at sites of past volcanic activity where moisture is trapped and heated by the energy in subterranean volcanic rocks. These rocks are rich in minerals, which are dissolved and carried to the surface in the super-hot water. Such places have long been exploited for the refreshing and healing properties of their mineral-laden springs.

"Old Faithful"
So called because it never fails to erupt on time, this fantastic geyser in Yellowstone National Park spurts a hot-water fountain 164 ft (50 m) into the air, approximately every 70 minutes.

The mineral aphthitalite

Crusty layers
As hot-spring water cools, thick, colorful mineral crusts form at the edges of pools and overflow channels. Likewise, crystal formations, notably sulfur, occur near steam vents.

Large, translucent crystals

Pure sulfur crystals

Simmering mud pot
Where hot-spring water mixes with rock particles broken down by acidic gases, bubbling basins of creamy mud are born, like this one in Iceland. The close-up (left) is of a mud pool in the Solfatara Crater near Naples, Italy.

"Morning Glory"
Another star of Yellowstone National Park is this pool, famous for the stunning colors of the tiny plants (algae) and bacteria living in its nutrient-rich waters.

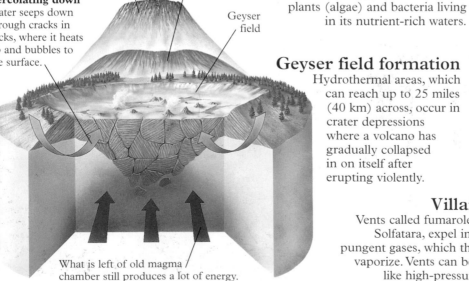

Past active volcano

Percolating down
Water seeps down through cracks in rocks, where it heats up and bubbles to the surface.

Erupted volcano sinking

Geyser field

Geyser field formation
Hydrothermal areas, which can reach up to 25 miles (40 km) across, occur in crater depressions where a volcano has gradually collapsed in on itself after erupting violently.

Yellow peril
Spiky sulfur crystals form around the vent entrance.

What is left of old magma chamber still produces a lot of energy.

Villainous odors
Vents called fumaroles, like this one at Solfatara, expel invisible plumes of pungent gases, which then condense and vaporize. Vents can be noisy, sounding like high-pressure steam engines.

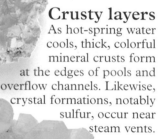

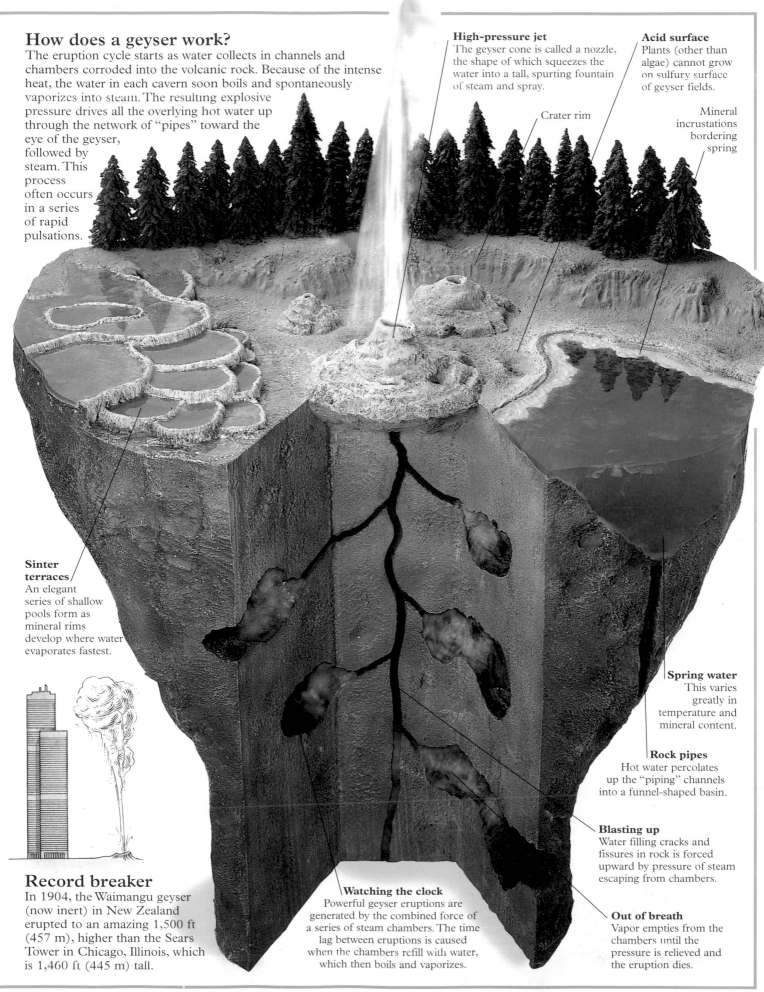

How does a geyser work?

The eruption cycle starts as water collects in channels and chambers corroded into the volcanic rock. Because of the intense heat, the water in each cavern soon boils and spontaneously vaporizes into steam. The resulting explosive pressure drives all the overlying hot water up through the network of "pipes" toward the eye of the geyser, followed by steam. This process often occurs in a series of rapid pulsations.

High-pressure jet
The geyser cone is called a nozzle, the shape of which squeezes the water into a tall, spurting fountain of steam and spray.

Acid surface
Plants (other than algae) cannot grow on sulfury surface of geyser fields.

Crater rim

Mineral incrustations bordering spring

Sinter terraces
An elegant series of shallow pools form as mineral rims develop where water evaporates fastest.

Spring water
This varies greatly in temperature and mineral content.

Rock pipes
Hot water percolates up the "piping" channels into a funnel-shaped basin.

Blasting up
Water filling cracks and fissures in rock is forced upward by pressure of steam escaping from chambers.

Record breaker

In 1904, the Waimangu geyser (now inert) in New Zealand erupted to an amazing 1,500 ft (457 m), higher than the Sears Tower in Chicago, Illinois, which is 1,460 ft (445 m) tall.

Watching the clock
Powerful geyser eruptions are generated by the combined force of a series of steam chambers. The time lag between eruptions is caused when the chambers refill with water, which then boils and vaporizes.

Out of breath
Vapor empties from the chambers until the pressure is relieved and the eruption dies.

Rivers of ice

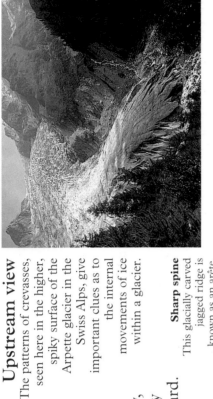

In addition to protruding like icy tongues from the polar ice caps, glaciers occur at high altitudes in milder regions. These are called valley, or alpine, glaciers. Originating in rounded "cirques," glaciers often combine to form a massive, sluggish flow. For a glacier to survive and grow, more snow must accumulate on its upper reaches than is lost by melting at the edges. This ongoing cycle drives the glacier forward. Meltwater pipes and chambers beneath a glacier help it slide over its bed, often in "surges." In Alaska, amazingly, glaciers have been seen to travel several miles in only a few days.

Upstream view
The patterns of crevasses, seen here in the higher, spiky surface of the Arpette glacier in the Swiss Alps, give important clues as to the internal movements of ice within a glacier.

Sharp spine
This glacially carved jagged ridge is known as an arête.

Snow blanket
Freshly fallen snow covers the upper parts of the glacier.

Medial moraine

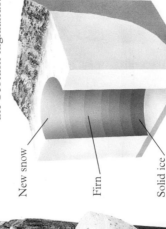

After the ice has gone
Glaciers deepen and straighten their host valleys into characteristic U-shaped troughs, like this one viewed from the summit of Cairn Gorm in the Scottish highlands.

Snow to ice
As new snow piles up on top of a glacier, the snow beneath it is slowly compacted. With repeated melting and refreezing, "firn" results. The ice at the base has had most of the air squeezed out of it.

New snow

Firn

Solid ice

Ice fall
Where there are steep drops in the underlying bedrock, the glacier ice breaks up into a series of huge, transverse, steplike crevasses.

Lateral moraine

Head of glacier in cirque

Deep fracture
A "bergschrund" crevasse forms as ice is pulled away from the back wall of the cirque under its own weight.

Steep walls
This typical Norwegian fjord is a deep trough carved by a glacier, then flooded by the sea after the ice retreated.

Hanging valley
Here the present glacier has cut right through an earlier valley. In some glacially formed landscapes, dramatic waterfalls result where a river flows over the edge of a hanging valley.

Emerging torrent
Meltwater carries huge amounts of finely ground rock material, as this stream at the snout of the Zinal glacier in Switzerland shows well.

Merging together
The outline of the smaller glacier is marked by rocks trapped in the ice.

Scraped clean
Bedrock surface is scoured and smoothed by boulders embedded in the slow-moving ice

Streams converge in meltwater pond.

Left behind
Ground moraine material deposited by the glacier as it retreats is molded into various lumpy landscape features.

Moulin

Different speeds
Curved crevasses show how the flow of ice is faster and closer to the surface in the middle of a glacier.

Meltwater chamber

Ice cave mouth

Three steps of a glacier
These models represent the beginning, middle, and end of a typical valley glacier made up of a major and a secondary flow. Rocky debris carried within the glacial ice, known as moraine, indicates where the flows join. Lateral moraine accumulates along the valley sides and terminal moraine at the snout, where large gravel lodges along the base.

Gaping chasm
Surface meltwater plunges down a moulin, or drainage shaft, which leads into tubes and chambers at the glacier's base.

Muddy end
Glacier snout is discolored by fine debris.

Ice continent

Antarctica is the Earth's southernmost and most inhospitable continent, with an average winter temperature of a blood-curdling −76°F (−60°C). Together with the Arctic, its northern twin, the Antarctic ice sheet locks away almost 90 percent of the world's freshwater into a permanent frozen reservoir. Changes in the size of the ice sheets, which may be many miles thick in places, are now monitored by satellites; these show that between summer and winter, ice sheets vary by as much as five times their own mass in extent. The coverage and depth of the ice is thought to have a distinct effect on the Earth's climate, and studies are now in progress to determine the nature of this relationship.

Permanent ice cover

South Pole

GREATER ANTARCTICA

LESSER ANTARCTICA

Antarctica
Unlike the Arctic, which is a vast oceanic ice sheet, Antarctica is a continent of solid rock ringed by ice. The thick ice at both poles is very old and preserves a record of past environments.

Tabletops
Some icebergs can be up to 150 miles (240 km) long and 70 miles (110 km) wide. Gargantuan tabular, or flat-topped, icebergs, like this one, break off the ice shelves lining the edges of the continent.

In the freezer
The thickness of the Antarctic ice cap has built up over thousands of years as fresh layers of snow have gradually been compacted. The ice slowly flows, or deforms, out toward the sea under its own weight, forming vast buoyant shelves lined by dramatic, sheer ice cliffs.

HMS *Endurance*, flagship vessel of the British Antarctic Survey

As icebergs are attacked by wave action, deep ice caves can often be created at the waterline.

Pack ice

Floating ice raft
During the short summer season, packs of crabeater seals are a common sight along Antarctic shorelines. Here a small group basks lazily in the sunshine on a drifting ice floe.

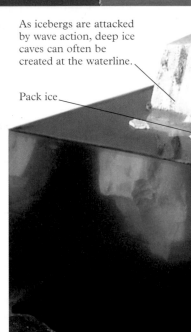

Basic necessity
Krill, shrimplike crustaceans just 2 in (5 cm) long, are a vital food source for whales, seals, penguins, and seabirds.

Ice sculptures
As icebergs melt and are eroded by the action of wind and waves, weird and wonderful shapes and patterns can be produced.

Head for heights
Icebergs can reach dizzying heights. One Arctic berg, spotted in 1958, was higher than St. Paul's Cathedral in London.

Blue glass
Some icebergs can appear completely blue as they reflect the water around them. Here the ice has been molded into what look like huge frosted-glass bottles.

Birth of an iceberg
Vast, icy pillar generates huge waves as it "calves" off the main shelf.

Polar ice may be many miles thick.

Jagged peaks
High mountaintops jutting through the surface of the ice cap are called nunataks.

Huge crevasses appear on surface of ice sheet as it moves and cracks internally.

Ice and rock material scrapes over bedrock as it moves.

Emperor penguins

Thermal gear
Penguins have tough feathers and thick blubber to keep out the Antarctic cold. Their teeming, noisy, summer breeding colonies are a spectacular sight.

More than two-thirds of an iceberg's bulk is hidden below water.

Seabed is littered with bouldery gravel and silt deposited by melting icebergs.

Ocean depths

Shrouded in mystery, the ocean floors remain largely unexplored. From the shallow edges, or shelves, of the continents, they descend dramatically, leveling off into ocean basins that may be up to 3.5 miles (6 km) below the surface. Oceanic trenches plunge even deeper – up to a staggering 7 miles (11 km). This strange undersea world conceals huge plains, mountain ranges, volcanoes, and canyons that dwarf anything seen on land. Whatever life exists has adapted to two extremes: the enormous pressure exerted by the weight of water above, and the total absence of light.

"Black smokers"
These strange features perch like chimneys on top of hydrothermal vents, cracks in the ocean floor where seawater gushes up, having been heated by hot volcanic rock below. First found in 1977, vents occur close to volcanic rifts in the seabed.

Super-hot water cools as it emerges.

Poisonous jets
The sulfurous water at vents is highly toxic, but wildlife has adapted uniquely by surviving on bacteria that flourish on the toxic compounds.

Molded mounds
Smokers, which can be up to 33 ft (10 m) tall, are built up by minerals dissolved in the gushing water. The minerals solidify and accumulate as the water cools.

Red-tipped tentacles
These giant tube worms were photographed at a vent near the Galapagos Islands in the eastern Pacific. Typical vent-site residents, they can be up to 10 ft (3 m) long. For food they depend on bacteria living inside their trunklike bodies, which they in turn supply with hydrogen sulfide and other chemicals extracted from the gaseous vent water.

Tube-worm tentacle

World under the waves

The continental shelves give way to continental slopes, or rises, down which huge amounts of sediment cascade in gulleys. The ocean floor terrain includes abyssal plains (vast areas of flat seabed), mountain ridges, and long rifts in the Earth's crust.

Continental shelf

Continental slope

Abyssal plain

Chain of peaked seamounts

Mid-ocean spreading ridge where rising lava cools to form new crust

Oceanic crust

Guyot (flat-topped seamount)

Deepest places on Earth
Chasmlike trenches mark the junction of crustal plates (pp. 10–11). Despite huge pressure, utter darkness, and freezing conditions, marine life such as sea cucumbers, anemones, and crustaceans still survive here in what is called the "hadal zone."

Seabed cushions
Lying near the deep-sea spreading ridges are fields of "pillow lava," molten rock that has oozed up through fissures in the ocean floor and then cooled.

Blind predator
The varied crustaceans living at vent sites are all blind. Here a spider crab scavenges in a clump of tube worms.

Vent architecture
Two smoker chimneys have fused together at their summits, forming an arch of solidified minerals.

Oasis of life
Alvin's powerful lights reveal the flourishing and diverse community in the warm water adjacent to smokers.

Deep-sea pioneers
The US submersible *Alvin*, seen here aboard its mother ship, carried the three scientists who first discovered the vent sites off the Galapagos Islands in 1977. Submersibles have to be ultra-strong to withstand enormous water pressure.

Snapped shut
In and around the tube-worm thickets lie giant mollusks (mussels and clams) up to 1 ft (30 cm) long.

Towering cliffs

Rocky coasts are a battleground between the attacking waves of the sea and the defending forces of the land. Sea cliffs, under attack at their bases, suffer frequent rockfalls, forming sheer faces. Eventually, the type of rock they are composed of will be revealed in their form – rock that is layered and jointed gives rise to dramatic stack and arch formations, while that formed from mud and gravel is eroded away rapidly, leaving little behind. Beaches are the result of eroded material accumulating at the shoreline; steep, narrow, "storm" beaches are common at the foot of sea cliffs.

Vertical cutoff
These plunging limestone cliffs stretch for miles and miles along the edge of the Nullarbor Plain, a vast, flat plateau in South Australia.

Mariner's friend
Standing proudly at the summit of jutting headlands, lighthouses like this one near Holyhead, in Anglesey, North Wales, warn sailors to steer clear of the rocks at the foot of cliffs.

Debris cone
Rockfalls contribute to slow process of cliff retreat.

Jagged edge
Cliff face is marked with crags and gulleys where boulders have fallen.

Storm waves eat away at cliff base.

Water spurts up through blowhole when sea is rough.

Cave mouth

Extended platform

1 Here the sea has already eroded its way deep into the cliffs of this imaginary coastline, eating away softer rock, and so sculpting an impressive arch.

Beaches form in more protected areas.

Gulls galore
Noisy seagulls are a typical sight flying over coastal cliffs.

Hard floor
Wave-cut shore platforms, or terraces, form at the base of the cliffs, where the sea's attack is most effective.

Arch roof slowly degrades.

Stack

2 As storm waves exert their erosive force, the cliff retreats over time. The root of the earlier sea arch has collapsed here, leaving a lone pillar, or stack. Another arch has appeared behind it.

Cove to bay
A cove begins to form where the sea finds a weak point in a cliff. It then carves out the less resistant rock behind the weak point. Slowly, a small cove is excavated into a wide, curving bay. Resistant rock left behind may form islands and protruding headlands.

Weak spot in cliff

Waves gradually wear down sides of cove.

Deposited rock debris forms beaches.

Tombolo in the making
Eroded material carried along the shore may link islands to the coast, creating a sandbar called a tombolo.

Tombolo

Deceptively docile
Now, at low tide, the sea is calm, belying the fact that at any minute the wind can stir up powerful waves that hurl themselves mercilessly at the cliffs.

Larger stones and pebbles

3 Now the coastline has moved backward some distance, and the only evidence of its original position is the two towering stacks. The cave and blowhole show that the present cliff is still being excavated by water action and cavitation by air trapped in the rocks.

First stack, continually being worn down

Gritty sand

Rocks to sand
Beyond the bouldery rocks right at the foot of a cliff, beach material gradually gets finer as the grains wear each other away.

Boulders carried away from beach by waves

Fine sand

Where cliffs once stood
Where cliffs once stood, wave-cut platforms of resistant rock often remain, as seen in the foreground of this stretch of coast near the Cape of Good Hope in South Africa.

Coral reefs

Colorful and swarming with life, coral reefs are the marine gardens of tropical oceans. Reefs result from the accumulation of limestone created by the hard outer skeletons of tiny animals called polyps. Although reefs can be very broad and plunge hundreds of feet deep, only their upper sections are alive, as polyps can only survive in warm, shallow water. The microscopic plants upon which they feed, called algae, are sensitive to the amount of sunlight penetrating the water; below a few feet, they cannot function. Reef conservation is a major ecological concern, since many are under threat from tourism and pollution.

Sleek and deadly
Graceful reef sharks stalk their prey in the plentiful hunting grounds of reef edges.

Green and humid
The steep sides of the island are covered with a lush blanket of tropical vegetation.

Volcanic cone
Layers of lava and ash from repeated eruptions build up.

Pacific paradise
Kayangell Atoll, in the Palau group of the Caroline Islands, is a typical ring-shaped coral atoll with verdant coral islands shielding a central, shallow lagoon.

Surface spurs
Deep channels allow the exchange of water and nutrients between a lagoon and the open ocean.

Young coral reef

1 A coral reef starts to grow in shallow waters around the fringes of a volcano rising above the ocean's surface.

Sloping down
The sides of the volcano descend toward the seabed.

Exotic species
Coral reefs are rich habitats teeming with a vast range of wildlife, including fish in all shades of colors.

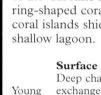

Emperor angelfish   **Royal Gramma**

2 As the surface of the volcano erodes and its base sinks into the ocean floor, the gap between it and the fringing coral reef widens into a lagoon. Meanwhile, the reef grows upward. This can also result from rising sea levels.

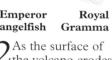

Maroon clownfish

Sandy lagoon

Orange sea fan

This gorgonian (horny) coral has a skeleton of long, branching arms that allow it to strain food from the water's waving currents.

Scuba playground

Plunging reef walls and caverns are perfect sites for divers to explore the extraordinary colors and shapes of coral formations.

Scallop shelters in a fold

Home for scallops

Rose coral is a leafy colony of many tiny animals growing on the seabed.

Tentacles trap food.

Mouth

Stomach cavity

Stony base of polyp skeletons

Green as lettuce
This reef sea slug owes its bizarre color to the algae that it eats.

Layer upon layer

Colonies of hard coral polyps are linked by a layer of soft tissue. They are hosts to single-celled algae, which they eat. They also catch plankton from the water.

Seaplane flying overhead

Marine park

Australia's Great Barrier Reef, the largest reef in the world, stretches for 1,260 miles (2,028 km) along the Queensland coast.

4 Now the flattened top of the volcano has vanished beneath the ocean's surface, and coral grows over it. Vegetation has gradually colonized the small atoll islands ringing the lagoon.

Queen angelfish

Reef wall

3 The process goes on as described, with small outcrops of coral appearing inside the lagoon. Where the surface of the reef is uncovered at low tides, fine material is gradually deposited until sandy islands are formed in patches.

Flame angelfish

Falls and rapids

Dramatic waterfalls and cascades, raging rapids, gaping canyons – these river features inspire awe as we ponder the powerful force of water. Spectacular falls most often occur where a river shoots over the edge of a plateau, a tablelike ledge of hard rock, crashing down onto a plain or valley beneath. Glistening cascades or turbulent rapids form where rivers are forced over and around obstructive outcrops or steps of resistant bedrock. Canyons are the result of strong river currents slowly eating away at bedrock, eventually digging deep channels.

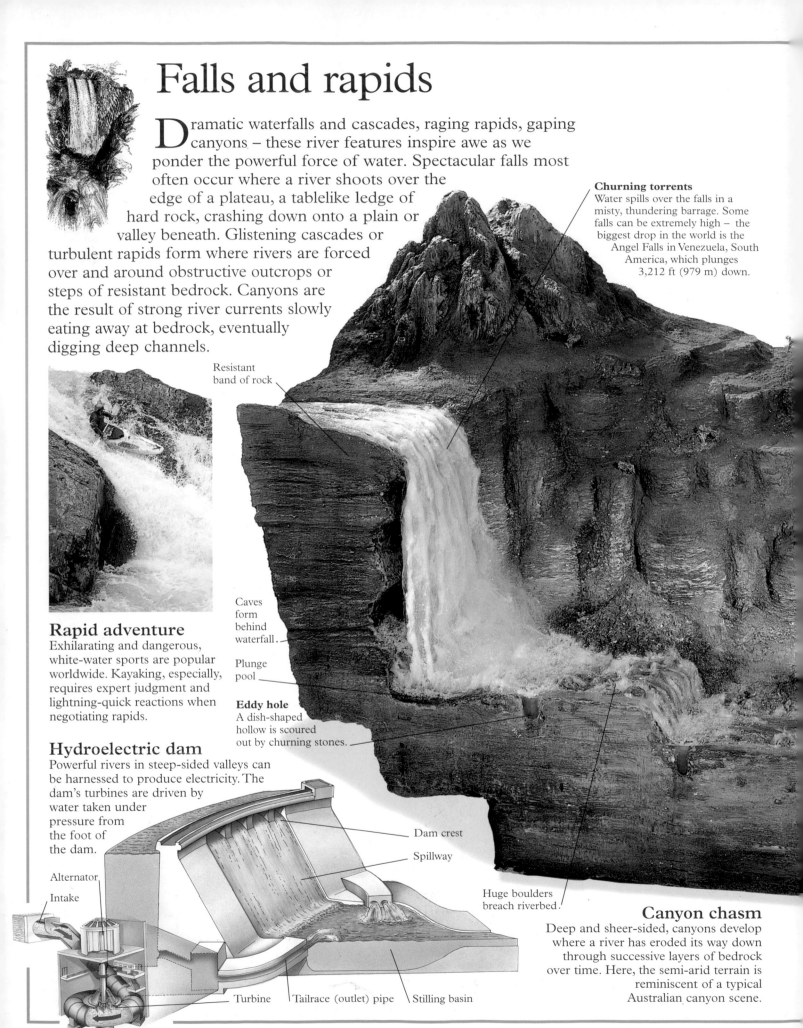

Churning torrents
Water spills over the falls in a misty, thundering barrage. Some falls can be extremely high – the biggest drop in the world is the Angel Falls in Venezuela, South America, which plunges 3,212 ft (979 m) down.

Resistant band of rock

Caves form behind waterfall

Plunge pool

Eddy hole
A dish-shaped hollow is scoured out by churning stones.

Rapid adventure
Exhilarating and dangerous, white-water sports are popular worldwide. Kayaking, especially, requires expert judgment and lightning-quick reactions when negotiating rapids.

Hydroelectric dam
Powerful rivers in steep-sided valleys can be harnessed to produce electricity. The dam's turbines are driven by water taken under pressure from the foot of the dam.

Alternator

Intake

Dam crest

Spillway

Huge boulders breach riverbed

Turbine   Tailrace (outlet) pipe   Stilling basin

Canyon chasm
Deep and sheer-sided, canyons develop where a river has eroded its way down through successive layers of bedrock over time. Here, the semi-arid terrain is reminiscent of a typical Australian canyon scene.

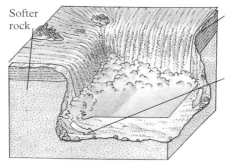

Softer rock

Edge of hard rock forms lip over which water pours.

Plunge pool
Rocks swirling around in the turbulent water gouge out a bowl-shaped depression at the foot of the falls.

Moving backward

Falls are constantly retreating upstream in a continuous cycle. Softer rock underlying a resistant top band is eroded away, forming a cavity with a rocky roof that eventually collapses.

Massive volume

At 355 ft (108 m) the Victoria Falls in Zimbabwe are not the highest in the world, but they carry the largest volume of water of any waterfall.

Flowing staircase

The Trappstegsforsen, or "step stream" cascade, flows through a forest in Swedish Lapland. It is a smaller-scale example of how bedrock structures can control a river's course, here converting it into a splendid series of watery terraces.

Fallen rock
Canyon walls are scarred by gulleys where rocks have fallen, leaving cones of boulders piled up at the river's edge.

Green edges
Small bushes and other plants grow among the rocks in the moist riverbank environment.

Red sandstone rock strata exposed

Only sparse vegetation exists on higher, and drier, surrounding land.

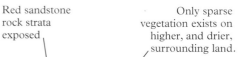

Mighty leaps

For salmon returning to their upstream spawning grounds, falls present the ultimate in acrobatic challenges.

Moist cover
Typical vegetation edging waterfalls and riverbanks in temperate zones include ferns and mosses.

Fern

White water
Rapids shoot over debris dams of huge boulders, with calmer water between each dam.

Limestone caves

Exploring a
lofty cavern

The landforms on and under the Earth's surface are related to the kind of rock from which they are formed. One very distinctive example occurs where water flows through limestone, which is made up of blocks, like bricks in a wall. Water slowly penetrates the joints between the blocks, and, because the rock is sensitive to attack by chemicals in the water, it gradually dissolves. Over time, powerful rivers can excavate vast subterranean cave systems, silent worlds of majestic and mysterious caverns, galleries, and deep, menacing shafts.

Birth of a pothole
Water gradually seeps through joints in the rock, dissolving rock and forming cracks that widen over time into potholes.

Cave dwellers
Bats often live in colonies and sleep during the day in the safety of dark caverns, emerging only at night to feed.

Lesser horseshoe bats

Amazing shapes
As well as pillar-shaped stalagmites and stalactites, many other bizarre and beautiful formations adorn caverns and galleries, including curtains and folds like these in Cox's Cave at Cheddar, Somerset, England.

Holes in the ground
Dramatic dolines, or sinkholes, like this one at Totes Gebirge, Austria, which is 22 yards (20 m) deep, are surface depressions caused by water dissolving the rock from above, or by cave roofs falling in.

Steep channel
carved by stream

Inside layers
Slicing through a stalactite reveals bands caused by sequences of mineral deposits. The lighter and darker colors of the bands indicate the varying amounts of impurities present in the deposits, the lightest being the most pure.

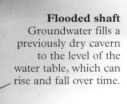

Flooded shaft
Groundwater fills a previously dry cavern to the level of the water table, which can rise and fall over time.

Down under
A typical limestone cave system is shown in this model. The hillside is characteristically bare – limestone offers little moisture and nutrients for lush vegetation. High up, the rock surface has been scraped clean by glacial action, forming a limestone pavement dissected by deep grooves.

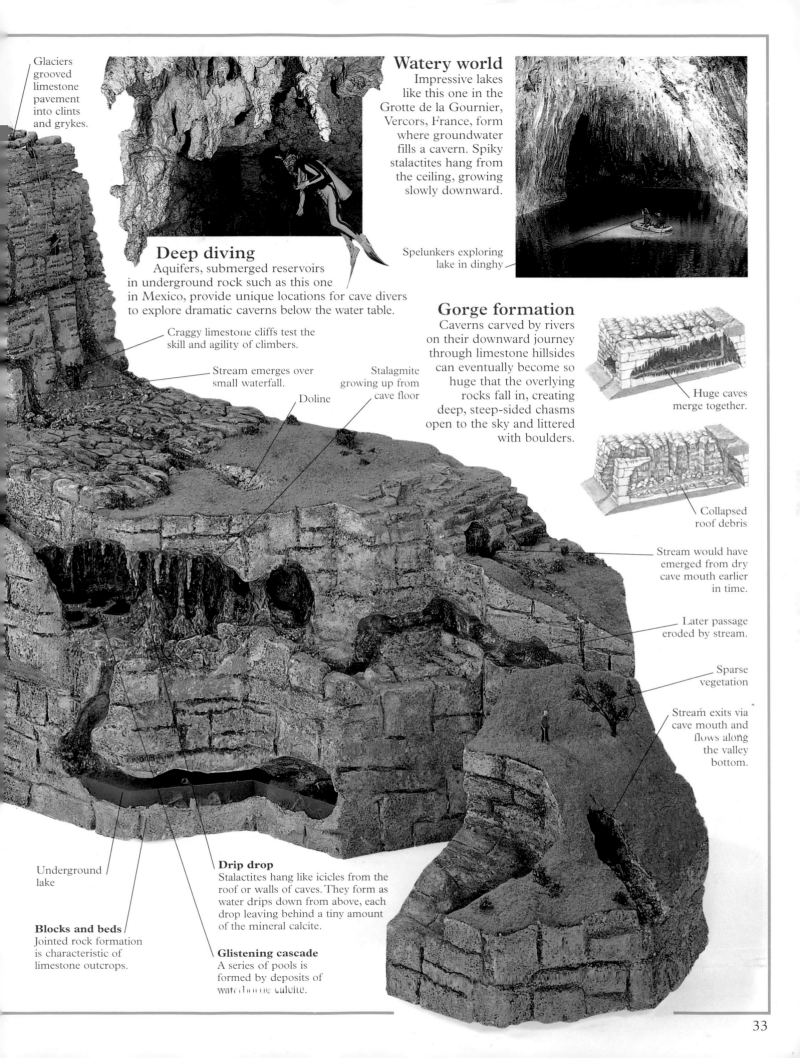

Glaciers grooved limestone pavement into clints and grykes.

Watery world
Impressive lakes like this one in the Grotte de la Gournier, Vercors, France, form where groundwater fills a cavern. Spiky stalactites hang from the ceiling, growing slowly downward.

Spelunkers exploring lake in dinghy

Deep diving
Aquifers, submerged reservoirs in underground rock such as this one in Mexico, provide unique locations for cave divers to explore dramatic caverns below the water table.

Craggy limestone cliffs test the skill and agility of climbers.

Stream emerges over small waterfall.

Doline

Stalagmite growing up from cave floor

Gorge formation
Caverns carved by rivers on their downward journey through limestone hillsides can eventually become so huge that the overlying rocks fall in, creating deep, steep-sided chasms open to the sky and littered with boulders.

Huge caves merge together.

Collapsed roof debris

Stream would have emerged from dry cave mouth earlier in time.

Later passage eroded by stream.

Sparse vegetation

Stream exits via cave mouth and flows along the valley bottom.

Underground lake

Blocks and beds
Jointed rock formation is characteristic of limestone outcrops.

Drip drop
Stalactites hang like icicles from the roof or walls of caves. They form as water drips down from above, each drop leaving behind a tiny amount of the mineral calcite.

Glistening cascade
A series of pools is formed by deposits of waterborne calcite.

Floodplains and deltas

As it travels, a river collects sediment from the rock and land near its source. Soon other flows, or tributaries, merge with it, forming a broad river basin containing a vast amount of muddy material. As the mass of water and suspended sediment reaches flatter ground, it slows down and wanders, or meanders. Without a strong enough current to carry it, some sediment drops. This sediment, or silt, will eventually build up into a floodplain, a low-lying area the river may still submerge after a heavy rainfall. Finally the river reaches the ocean, where it loses all its force, dropping the rest of its load of sediment. Here the material forms a delta, an area of swampy land.

During the 19th century, sailing down the Nile on a dhow like this was a popular tourist activity.

Stagnant water spreads over a wide area.

Boggy wetlands
Marshes and swamps form where rivers flow over low-lying land. Waterlogged and overgrown, they are a haven for wildfowl in particular.

War against water
All great rivers are prone to floods. To protect people and property from this risk, artifical banks, or levees, and a complex series of water control mechanisms are often built, such as seen here along the Mississippi River.

Steamy tropics
This luxuriant cypress swamp near Fort Myers in Florida is typical of the low-lying coastline bordering the Gulf of Mexico. These are important habitats, thriving with an abundance of aquatic plants and wildlife.

Sharp teeth
Alligators are among the most feared residents of swamplands, thanks to their silent approach and gaping jaws.

Raised banks of distributaries are called levees.

Mediterranean Sea

Nile delta

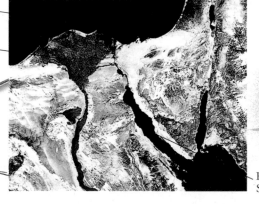

Red Sea

River mouth

Diverse uses
The papyrus reed, which grows extensively along the Nile valley and in the Nile delta, was used by the ancient Egyptians to make everything from writing parchment to simple boats.

Head of the Nile
The Nile River in Egypt flows through the Egyptian desert toward its wide, arc-shaped delta. Since ancient times, its annual flooding has enabled people to prosper along its banks. Without the Nile, the mighty pharoahs would never have existed.

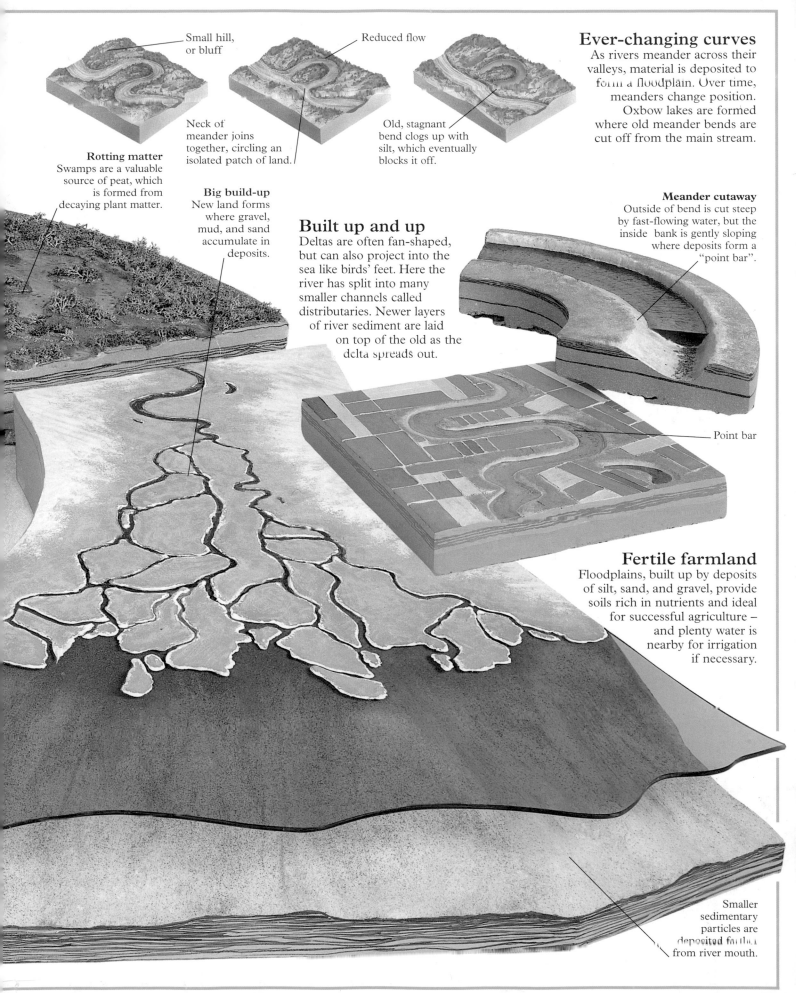

Small hill, or bluff

Reduced flow

Ever-changing curves
As rivers meander across their valleys, material is deposited to form a floodplain. Over time, meanders change position. Oxbow lakes are formed where old meander bends are cut off from the main stream.

Rotting matter
Swamps are a valuable source of peat, which is formed from decaying plant matter.

Neck of meander joins together, circling an isolated patch of land.

Old, stagnant bend clogs up with silt, which eventually blocks it off.

Big build-up
New land forms where gravel, mud, and sand accumulate in deposits.

Built up and up
Deltas are often fan-shaped, but can also project into the sea like birds' feet. Here the river has split into many smaller channels called distributaries. Newer layers of river sediment are laid on top of the old as the delta spreads out.

Meander cutaway
Outside of bend is cut steep by fast-flowing water, but the inside bank is gently sloping where deposits form a "point bar".

Point bar

Fertile farmland
Floodplains, built up by deposits of silt, sand, and gravel, provide soils rich in nutrients and ideal for successful agriculture – and plenty water is nearby for irrigation if necessary.

Smaller sedimentary particles are deposited farther from river mouth.

Desert lands

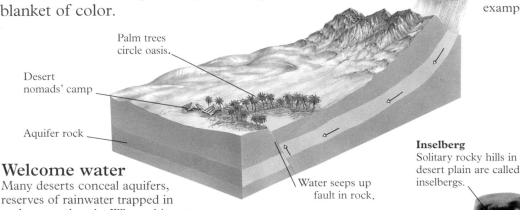

Arid and desolate, deserts are full of surprises. For example, while most occur in the hot, tropical areas of the world, some also exist in colder, mountainous

Ships of the desert

regions. Formed where more rainfall evaporates than falls, most deserts feature rocky uplands and barren plains rather than great "seas" of sand. When rains do come to desert lands, flash floods can occur, bringing seeds that have lain dormant in the ground for many years suddenly into bloom, transforming the dry landscape into a blanket of color.

Desert rose
Intriguing petal-shaped crystals like this form when gypsum dust dissolves in rainwater or groundwater inside sand dunes.

Pyramid stone
Even small stones and pebbles are shaped and varnished by wind blasting sand over them. This three-sided example is called a dreikanter.

Palm trees circle oasis.

Desert nomads' camp

Aquifer rock

Water seeps up fault in rock.

Welcome water
Many deserts conceal aquifers, reserves of rainwater trapped in underground rocks. Where this water reaches the surface, an oasis, or desert pond, appears, and plants can grow.

Hamada
Hostile desert plain strewn with small rocks or gravel is called a hamada.

Inselberg
Solitary rocky hills in desert plain are called inselbergs.

Rock arch
The wind sculpted this impressive formation from a protruding fin of rock.

Tapering walls
The skirt, or pediment, of the rocky upland has deep gulleys gouged out by the infrequent, but heavy, rains.

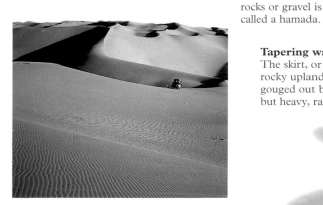

Spines and ripples
Prevailing winds shape the ergs, or sand seas, of the African Sahara into massive dune fields. Pictured here are long, narrow "seif" dunes; other forms are crescent- and star-shaped.

Shifting sands
Sand dunes are constantly on the move, blown in the same direction as the wind (blue arrow). This cross-section shows how old dune structures are overlaid and compacted by younger ones.

Gulleys and fans
Rocky outcrops like this one in Mungo National Park, Australia, are often scarred by deep gashes carved by rainwater. At their bases lie fan-shaped deposits of mud and silt.

Desert tombstones

This field of sand-blasted rock pinnacles is in Namburg National Park, Australia. The wind has worn down the outer layers of rock, leaving only columns and plinths of harder material. The effect is one of a silent, scorching graveyard.

Barrel cactus

Spikes deter predators.

Water bearers

Desert cacti conserve water by storing it in their fleshy tissue. Shallow roots spread out to absorb whatever rain or dew there is.

Water-storing tissue

Dry wadi
River channel carved by torrents of rainwater during flash floods.

Rock strata clearly visible in cliff face

Pinnacles of snow

High-altitude, or mountain, deserts, like the Atacama desert in Chile, are dry wildernesses where all moisture is locked in ice. Here, snow has frozen into spikes and pillars, awaiting the summer sun.

Desert plateau
Upland outcrops are gradually shrinking. The encircling cliffs are being worn down by a combination of wind, sand, extreme temperature variations, rainwater, and chemical processes.

Fallen boulders litter dry riverbed.

Fast mover
Desert creatures have adapted to the environment in amazing ways. This lizard's long claws have a fringe of scales to stop it from sinking into the sand.

Mesa

Butte

Towers and tables

The striking mesas and buttes, isolated flat-topped hills or mountains, of Monument Valley, Arizona, are all that remain of a vast plateau that has steadily eroded away.

Buried treasure

A priceless treasure trove of precious rare metals and dazzling gems, as well as an infinite variety of semiprecious stones and crystalline formations, lies hidden in rocks deep beneath the Earth's surface. Ever more ingenious ways have been devised to exploit this resource of mineral riches, by mining and quarrying, panning and dredging, in order to create beautiful decorative objects and means of exchange.

The Great Gold Rush drove many to search for gold in California and in Australia, despite harsh conditions.

Turquoise blue
This decorative stone, made up of many crystals, has been prized since early times for its unique color, which comes from copper and traces of iron.

Lustrous opal
Precious opal can form either in sedimentary rock or inside gas bubbles in volcanic rock. Here it is concealed inside a nodule of iron.

Opal

Mined out
Australia dominates the world opal market. Opals are usually milky white or black, shot through with iridescent blue, green, yellow, or red. This picture shows miners working a rock seam at the Coober Pedy mine in South Australia.

In layers
Faint bands reveal where the agate crystals have formed at different stages.

Waxy luster

Jadeite

Rare jade
Jade is the common name for both jadeite and nephrite. The former is more rare. Both are valued the world over for their toughness, which is perfect for delicate carving work.

Hidden beauty
This geode, or cavity within a rock, is lined with agate crystals.

Ready for work
The stone can now be cut and polished into gemstones.

Cavity with a difference
This specimen from Brazil shows a band of perfect crystals that formed inside a gas pocket (geode) within a cooling volcanic rock. Stones formed in this way can vary greatly in color depending on the minerals and chemicals present.

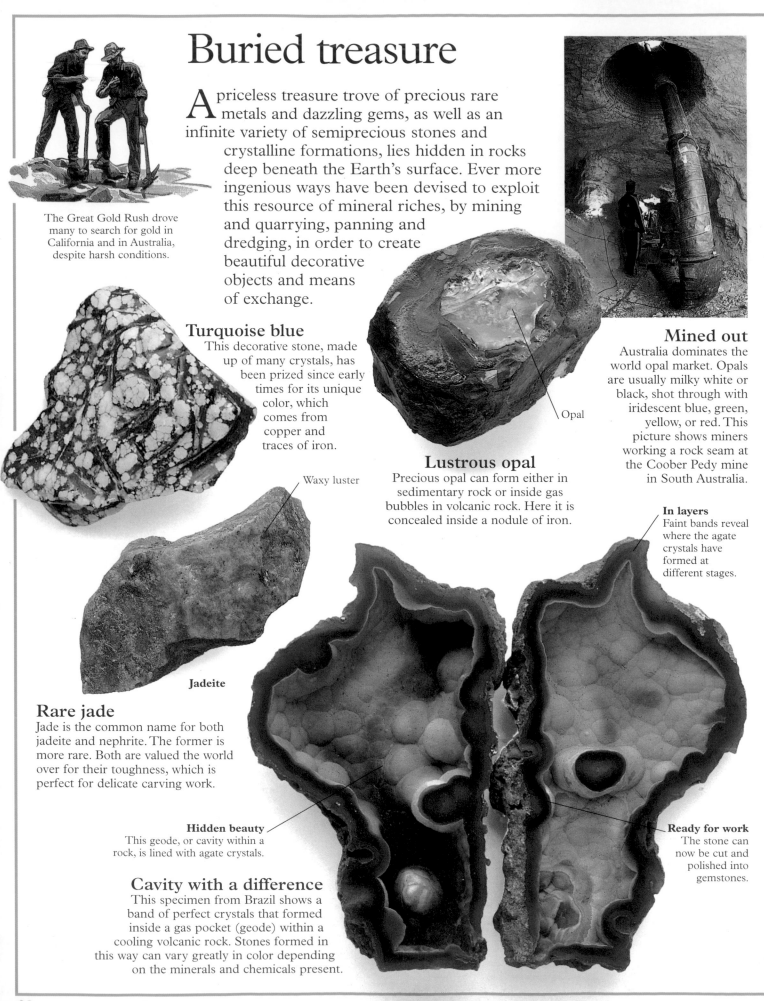

"The Big Hole"

This deep chasm is an old diamond mine in Kimberley, South Africa. South Africa is a major supplier of diamonds, and is home to De Beers, the firm that regulates the world diamond market.

Kashmir blue

Like ruby, sapphire is a variety of the mineral corundum. Sapphire describes a blue stone like the one above, but other colors include yellow, pink, and golden.

Ruskin's ruby

Donated to the Natural History Museum in London by the philosopher John Ruskin in 1887, this Burmese ruby crystal possesses a richness of color inherent in the highest quality gems.

Hard nut
This diamond is embedded in a lump of volcanic rock.

Diamond

The strength and durability of diamonds, along with their great luster and "fire," make them the most prized jewels in the world.

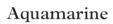

Aquamarine

This blue-green variety of beryl takes its name from the color of the sea. Beryl has been mined since ancient times, and also comes in yellow (heliodor) and pink (morganite) varieties.

Emerald crystal

Granite

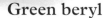

Swirling action

Gold can be found in the beds of rivers and streams. This 1908 painting shows a prospector panning for heavy grains and nuggets.

Rich veins

Gold is valued both for jewelry and some industrial processes, and even dentistry. It is often found in incrustations in veins of quartz.

Green beryl

Known as emerald, this is the most famous of beryl varieties. Spanish invaders first came across emeralds in the early 1500s among the treasures of the Incas of Peru and the Aztecs of Mexico.

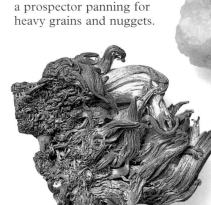

Platinum

This precious and malleable metal is now more valuable than gold.

Laborious process
A worker carts off the gold ore to be crushed; the residue will then be smelted.

Light-sensitive metal

Silver is currently used for many purposes, including on photographic films and paper. One of the first rare metals to be discovered, it is prone to tarnishing, which may explain why it has never been as valuable as gold.

Danger zone

Early gold mining was labor-intensive and the mine shafts were hazardous places to work, with poor ventilation and the constant threat of collapse.

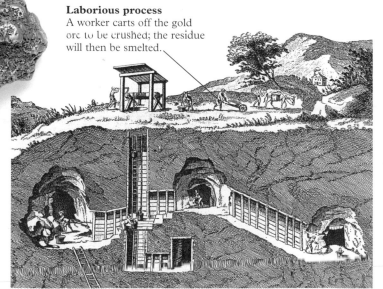

Caring for the Earth

The Earth is not large and its resources not infinite – it cannot survive as it is if we exploit it beyond measure. Already at almost 6 billion, global population is rising by 120 million each year. As a result, energy consumption is increasing, as is the amount of industrial and agricultural waste created. If the Earth is to survive, we must learn to nurture our planet. Use of energy and raw materials must be carefully planned. Waste disposal, especially of toxic substances, must be made safe, so we stop polluting our land and oceans. We must also protect the Earth's great abundance of natural habitats and wildlife for future generations to enjoy.

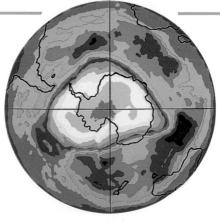

Window over Antarctica
The Earth's ozone layer protects us from harmful solar radiation. It is not certain what causes the "hole" in this layer (the pink area in the satellite image above) that occurs over Antarctica in spring. However, pollution in the atmosphere has been suggested.

Arctic garbage dump
Refuse from industrialized zones is washed up on remote Arctic coasts, demonstrating the global nature of sea pollution. Plastic, especially, is not easily broken down by natural processes, and will pollute the environment for many years.

Dried-out former seabed

An unquenchable thirst
This fishing boat in Uzbekistan, central Asia, has been stranded as the Aral Sea has receded. Over the last 30 years, so much river water that used to enter the lake has been diverted for irrigation that it has shrunk to half its former size.

Raw sewage
Direct discharge into rivers and seas is still a common way of disposing of sewage. Tighter laws controlling water quality, however, are gradually changing this practice.

Encroaching deserts
Where grasslands are under pressure from soil erosion, over-grazing, and climatic fluctuations, the need for soil conservation is acute. The Sahel region of Africa, bordering the southern edges of the Sahara desert, is particularly under threat; in some areas, the desert has advanced 220 miles (350 km) in just 20 years.

Bare plains
In typical areas of desertification, most of the sparse tree cover has been felled for fuel, which exposes the topsoil.

One big cover-up

Modern landfill methods of garbage disposal are carefully designed to prevent groundwater contamination as well as build-up of flammable gases. Any toxic substances, together with rainwater (this solution is called leachate), are pumped out of a pit.

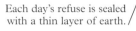

Natural landscape cover

Leachate pool

Pipes around site monitor groundwater quality.

Network of pipes allows dangerous gases to escape.

Each day's refuse is sealed with a thin layer of earth.

Pumping station
Shape of pit allows leachate to percolate along a loose gravel layer toward a central sump. From here it is pumped out and transported elsewhere for safe and effective disposal.

Pit lining

Layers of compacted earth

Gravel layer

Thick, waterproof plastic sheeting

Driven by the wind
Wind turbines are the successors of the traditional windmill, their blades rotating like huge propellors.

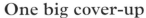

Jungle butterflies from South America

Gardens of Eden
Rain forests support a huge diversity of plants and wildlife. These ecosystems must be preserved and new forest created.

The search for renewable energy

In view of the Earth's dwindling fossil fuel reserves, new sources of energy must be found. Power can be generated by the wind (left), the tides, the Sun (solar power), and volcanic underground heat, as in Iceland (right).

River restoration
Over the last ten years, major efforts have been made to rejuvenate river and stream environments in industrial zones.

Slag (metal waste) heaps

New, winding river course created.

River area widened.

Gravel laid to encourage fish and water beetles to breed and new food chains to be created.

Trees and shrubs planted along banks.

Under threat
The Earth's most precious habitats are its tropical forests, but they are shrinking rapidly. Trees are felled for farmland or by logging companies. New logging methods, including replanting and other effective forest management techniques, are gradually being introduced around the world.

Forest floor provides plentiful food.

Glossary

Earth's insides exposed

A

Abyssal plain The deep, flatter areas of the ocean floors, often covered with scattered lumps, or nodules, of the metallic element manganese.

Algae Simple-structured plants that may be minute or huge seaweeds. Algae contain chlorophyll and manufacture their own food using sunlight.

Alternator An electrical device that creates an alternating current, a current that rapidly changes direction.

Aquifer A layer of rock trapping water underground.

Arctic The ice-covered area surrounding the North Pole.

B

Bacteria A large group of usually single-celled micro-organisms.

Bedrock Solid rock layers beneath the soil and surface cove of the Earth.

C

Canyon A narrow, steep-sided gorge, often formed by river erosion.

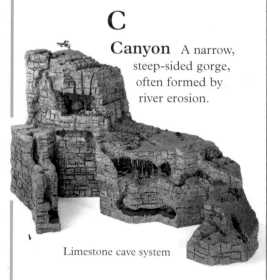

Limestone cave system

Clints and grykes Eroded ridges and grooves in limestone surfaces.

Cavitation An effect in which bubbles form and collapse in very fast-flowing water, causing rapid variations in pressure and resulting in considerable erosion and pitting.

Continental drift
Horizontal movements of the Earth's crust responsible for the present arrangement of the continents. Theory first published in 1915 by the German meteorologist Alfred Wegener (1880–1930).

Crevasse A deep crack or split in the surface of a glacier or ice sheet.

Crustaceans Animals with an external shell split into segments.

Four steps in the making of a coral atoll

D

Distributary Small channel on a river delta taking water from a main river to lakes or the sea.

Doldrums A belt of low atmospheric pressure surrounding the equator. Mariners used to dread the doldrums because their vessels could be becalmed for lengthy periods.

F

Fissure A crack in the side of a volcano through which lava escapes. The term also refers to a crack in any surface.

Fossil fuels Fuels that occur naturally and are formed from the decomposition of prehistoric organisms, including natural gas, crude oil, and coal.

G

Gastropod A type of mollusk, or shell-dwelling animal, often with a coiled shell – a snail for example.

Great Barrier Reef This lies off Australia's northeastern coast, and is the longest coral reef in the world. It has formed over some 800 million years, and is home to more than 400 types of coral and 1,500 species of fish.

Great Gold Rush This most famous gold rush occurred after gold was first discovered in California in 1848 by John Marshall. People flocked from the eastern United States and Europe in search of their fortunes. A similar rush took place in the wake of gold being discovered in Australia in 1851. Further gold rushes happened in later years and also in Canada, New Zealand, and South Africa.

Guyot A mountain on the ocean bed with a characteristic flat top that was once an island.

H

Hanging valley A tributary valley that enters its main river valley high up on one side, often creating a waterfall.

L

Limestone A calcium-rich rock often formed where fresh- or saltwater has evaporated or where shelled animals have died and accumulated on sea and lake beds.

River falls and rapids

M

Mineral An inorganic substance with a simple chemical form. Minerals are found in combinations in rocks.

Mollusks Invertebrate animals with shells.

Moulin A vertical pipe or shaft carrying water and rocks from the surface to the bed of a glacier.

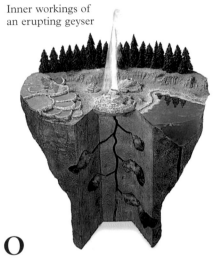

Inner workings of an erupting geyser

O

Ocean trench The deep troughs or valleys on the ocean floor. The deepest trenches occur at subduction zones, where oceanic and continental crustal plates converge.

Ores Metal-bearing rocks that can be mined and then processed to extract pure metal.

P

Panning Technique for separating grains of valuable mineral ores from riverbed sand and gravel by washing the material in a pan using a swirling action.

Plankton Very small (often microscopic) organisms that float in marine and freshwater environments. They may be animal, plant, or bacterial in origin.

Pumice A very light volcanic rock that water can easily penetrate, formed as steams and gases escaped from cooling lava.

Q

Quartz A common, usually glassy mineral formed from silicon and oxygen. Pulverized quartz makes up the bulk of sand.

R

Richter scale System for measuring the intensity, or magnitude, of an earthquake, based upon readings taken from a seismograph, which records ground motion. Named after the US seismologist Charles Richter (1900–1985), who developed it in 1935.

S

Sahara The world's largest desert, stretching more than 3,410 miles (5,500 km) east to west across North Africa and almost 1,240 miles (2,000 km) north to south). It is almost totally barren apart from scattered oases and the land adjacent to the Nile River.

Sand dune A massive accumulation of sand, blown and shaped by the wind into a hill or ridge.

Sandstone A rock formed from grains of sand cemented together by silica or calcium carbonate.

Satellite Man-made devices that continuously orbit the Earth in space. They have many uses, including communications, weather forecasts, marine and aircraft navigation, and keeping track of military exercises on the ground.

Slice through a blasting volcano

Solar radiation Energy received from the Sun, which drives the Earth's weather and climatic circulation. The energy is generated by nuclear reactions taking place inside the Sun itself. Amazingly, the entire population of the Earth only uses as much energy in one year as the Sun delivers to the Earth in under an hour.

T

Temperate zone A mid-latitude zone of the Earth, away from polar and equatorial areas, which is marked by warm and cool seasons.

Tributary A river or stream that feeds its water into a larger river or river system.

Tropics The region of the Earth centered on the equator, lying between 23.5° latitude N and S, and characterized by hot weather throughout the year.

W

Wadi A dry river channel in a desert area. It contains water only after heavy rainfall.

Black smokers in the ocean depths

Index

Acknowledgments

The publisher would like to thank: BBC Visual Effects, for their enthusiasm in making the models: Andrew David, Malcolm James, Mike Tucker, Colin Mapson, Alan Marshall, Alison Jeffrey, Nick Kool

Author's consultant: Dr. John French, Geography Department, University College London

Design assistance: Rachael Dyson, Iain Morris, Salesh Patel, Susan St. Louis, Jason Gonzalez, Emma Bowden

Editorial assistance: Julie Ferris

Photoshop retouching: Bob Warner and Oblong Box

Visualization: Martyn Foote

Illustrations: 8bl Peter Bull Art Studio; 9br Colin Salmon; 11cr, br, 14l, 18bl, 20br, 25tr, 30bl (turbine by Rick Blakeley), 35t, 36c Mike Saunders; 8tr Richard Ward; 9tr, 12tr, 19bl, 23tr, 29cl, 41tr, bl John Woodcock; 11cl David Ashby; 10c, 15br, 36bl Richard Bonson;16l , 31tl Colin Rose; 12–13 (except 12tr) Will Giles & Sandra Pond; 22tr Luciano Corbella; 33cr Nick Hall

Additional models: 10 Dave Donkin; 14–15, 36–37, 41br Donks Models; 24–25, 34–35 Peter Griffiths

Picture Credits
Key: l=left, r=right, t=top, c=center, a=above, b=below

Nick Clifford: 20cr; 21tl **Mary Evans Picture Library:** 16tl; 38tl; 39br; 39cl **Geoscience:** 17tr; 18crb; 32bl; 33tr; 34cla **Robert Harding Picture Library:** / Michael Botham 26cl; 20tr; 20cl; 32cl; 39tl **The Image Bank:** 10br; /Jeff Hunter 29tl; /Stefano Scato 29cr **Frank Lane Picture Agency:** /D. Fleetham/ Silvestris 28tr; /Mark Newman 30cl; /W. Wisniewsk 23tr; 31tc; 34cl; 40cr **Mansell Collection:** 8tl **Oxford Scientific Films:** /David Curl 26tr; /Ben Osborne 22cl, 23tl; /Richard Packwood 18cla **Photo © Jerry Young:** 34cr **Planet Earth:** /John R. Bracegirdle 27br; /John Fawcett 18tr;

21tr; /Robert Hessler 24cl; 25c; /Jan Jove Johansson 31tr; 36clb; 37br; /Doug Perrine 33tl; Jonathon Scott 22bl; /William Smithey 25cr; 27br; /Verena Tunnicliffe 25cl **Science Photo Library:** 10cl; 10-11; /Martin Bond 41cl; /Douglas Faulkner 28cl; 34bc; /Simon Fraser 37cra; 40c; 40cl; 41c; /Gordon Garradd 36br; /John Mead 37tl; /Peter Meizel 15tr, 15cr; 38tr; /Nasa 8clb; /David Parker 14tr; /Roger Ressmeyer/Starlight 16tr; /US Geological Survey 15tl; /John Wells 40tl **Frank Spooner Pictures:** 17br

Index: Marian Dent